# Benediction

poems by
Maya Imani Jones

*For the lives interrupted*

# Contents

# *Introduction*

     *Benediction* is a collection of poems about life interrupted. From 2016 until 2024, grief came to her on a platter. Losing at least one family member annually, radiating heartbreak, losing the majority of her previous creative work, and graduating as an artist in the midst of some little pandemic, she was isolated in what seemed to be an endless buffet of absence. Throughout this process, she realized she was never destined to follow familiar paths. No matter how hard she tried the pathways to success family and colleagues crafted to guide her through trying times, it was the submission to the unknown that ultimately brought her through. These poems reflect those years of working through endless interruption and rediscovering her voice. Let *Benediction* serve as a blessing to grieve, find joy, and begin again.

*For Grieving*

## Artist Aphasia

Numb.
> *What words could I even-*

Say something
> *They keep looking at you to*

SAY SOMETHING
> *Uh*

Higher
> *UMMM*

They can't hear you
> *They're not listening to-*

Try Harder
> *I don't know-*

Say SOMETHING
> *I'm just-*
> *Breathe*

You can still Breathe
For now the air is still free
Inhale
Exhale
Find it
The words
It's in their faces
They are waiting for you to-
> *Say something*

> *Alright*

## Bird Song

I miss my calloused hands from the monkey bars.
I miss the stabbing of wood chips in thick knit white wool stockings.
I miss the gnarled knotty bole of the hallowed out magic tree.
I miss when little girls could be birds migrating south
escaping the frigid truths of femininity.

I miss striped candy straws
sucking nectar from halved lemons
Sweet and soured
Honeysuckle harmonies.
I miss the black top heat
Where the only divisions were the boxes
of four square and ballroom dancing.

I was lucky to grow up in the woods
Where bog wading and bird watching were the norm
Where creeks were for streaming and not a yet symptom
of simple motor function.
We were still figuring that out
We were still drawing our bodies out.

I miss how I felt before the missing.
Before my taste buds were bittered by the yearning for belonging
Knowing I was somehow out of place
Negative space

Always in reference
In comparison, in competition
An anxious academic tongue tied.

I wish I could remember my bird song.
My voice, my timbre
Before influence Imperial became cerebral
Code switching became armor
Respectability's politics became the ruling party.
I wish I could feel the jolt of discovery
Without the resistance of expectations
The dampening of disappointments.

I miss not knowing how the world works.


Blissful


Ignorant of prejudiced glances
And snide commentary.
I miss when community was a classroom of monarch butterflies
fresh from their cocoons.
Orange and black wings filling the skies instead of prison cells.
The caw of the crow was music instead of an omen.
The coo of the dove was a celebration of a new day instead of a
mourning for the last

I miss when the pain in my hands were from the monkey bars.
Now they bleed from holding together
the splintered factions of myself
Jagged little pieces of dissonant melodies.

I wish I learned to play double dutch while ropes were still for
jumping.
I wish I remembered how to sing my bird song.

## GPS

Antagonising obelisk pulsates
a homing beacon
Leading you,
maybe,
To learned oasis


Horizon omnipresent

To stay or to go?


Into
the great deletion


arid desertscape

## Fort Worth

I don't think I've fought for my dreams since I decided to chase them
I've fallen through trap doors, taken side quests
Have rolled 1 One too many times

I've been playing defense
Blocking shots to my ego and my liver
Identify and eliminate, Zone, 1v1
A 300 pound lineman lady in waiting for the ball to snap

I've reinforced the walls I've built
A Brick and Mortar Mortal
Propagandized my capabilities, confidences
Secured my insecurities with bolts and now I'm screwed
My fortress is built

A fortress of self worth
Identity theft
A fraudulent, Tax evasion
I don't think I've paid my dues
Just my debts, interest accrued

And my dreams
Intangible mist
What are they worth when I'm living yesterday's nightmare?
What am I worth on the offensive?

Fortification is the best option
Lest I am faced with the reality
That I really am That Girl

How would I wield all that power?

**Lazarus**

Beggar Beggar Beggar
Gravedigger Digger
Butcher Butcher
Leper
What should I do with my decaying dreams?
How do I get the meat to not spoil
The thoughts not to rot
The passion not to poison me

Butcher Butcher
I've put it on ice
It's been crystalizing
In the freezer burnt reaches of my brain
My dreams are sitting next to
The numbers 32 and 36
A pre pandemic promise
And a pint of ice cream

Beggar Beggar Beggar
Are your prayers getting answered
Is there a prime position to hear our pleas
I've been shouting into the void
Hoping for the reverb to point me in the right direction
General Vicinity stopped giving me orders
And Silence is the hardest to answer

Leper
How are you holding it all together
When everyone runs,
Ooze and Ahh at you
When you are falling apart at the seams
Can you continue to dream
When you have been forsaken

Gravedigger Digger
Let me lend you a hand
I must lay my brainchild down
Mummified memories
The sands of time caressing
his casket
Ashes to ashes,
decisions to dust.

The death of a Dream
Its decay nourishes the soil
Failure as fertilizer
Mistakes for manure
Lessons as lesions
That itch while they heal

Beggar Beggar Beggar
Gravedigger Digger
Butcher Butcher
Leper
Will you be the pallbearers for my decaying dreams?

**U=**

In physics, potential energy is the energy held by an object because of its position relative to other objects, stresses within itself, its electric charge, or other factors.
Often denoted with the capital letter U

U=
M times G Times H
Gravitational
½ times K times x squared
Elastic
Negative M times B
Magnetic
½ multiplied by C multiplied by V squared
Electricity

But what's the formula for putting together people
What is the derivative for friends turned family
Family turned enemy
Enemy to friend turned lover now stranger
Who has written out this perfect proof of potential
How has it slipped into each glance
Every soft spoken word
Whispered instead of shouted

Potential

U=
little i
idealized imaginary scenarios
Cupid's bow and arrow drawn
What's the probability
It hits the intended target and doesn't leave both parties wounded

Heavy is the head that wears the crown
dripping in joules
as gravity pulls you down from the pedestal I've placed you on

What's the chemical make up of the tears that fall
in darkness as you sleep peacefully beside me
Salt, Water, Protein,
Mucus, Serotonin, Manganese,
Prolactin, Potassium, Potential

What was it that drew you in
My positive energy to
Your negative
When will it end
My devastating attraction to these nihilistic men

What makes too much positivity so repulsive?

Was it stress self inflicted that pushed you away?
Or external factors as resistors that dimmed your light?

Who gave you the right
to drain me like batteries
A thief of energy
Leaving me to solder sober emotions like wires exposed and frayed
Still I wonder
What would have happened if you stayed

The Possibility of Potentially
Pouring into each other comfortably
Intimately
Infinitely
U=

## Boredom is a privilege

Boredom is a privilege
It's best friends with Ignorance and Youth
And the mother of Imagination
2nd cousins to Creativity
Enemy of Productivity
And Victim to Capitalism

Boredom's got a new best friend
It walked into their life some years back
around the same time as Responsibility
And never quite left.
Unfortunately for them this was a
Parasitic partnership

Apathy,
Younger Sibling to the twins
Depression and Anxiety,
(All three the daughters of
White Capitalist Society)
Is never seen too far from Boredom.
It holds a tight leash
The friendship bracelets cause lacerations.

See Apathy was the jealous type
She wanted Boredom's freedoms

Their ability to transform and daydream.
Their openness was intimidating.
So Apathy called for backup
to cut off Boredom's community.

Education and Experience
came to take Ignorance away
And Time diluted Youth
Creativity was relocated
To live with Productivity
Under Capitalism's roof

That just leaves three
Apathy, Imagination, and Responsibility
Tethered to her mother
Imagination was the hardest to remove
But filling feeds with a steady streams
Of others fulfilling Boredom's wildest dreams
Left Imagination malnourished and waning

Time came by
Piling more onto Responsibility's plate.
A wobbling tower of worries.
Depression and Apathy
Lent a hand to carry the load
While Anxiety read Imagination
Bedtime stories

Boredom is a privilege
High maintenance and fickle
A thorny rose bush needing
Tender tending,
Nutrient rich soil
And ample space to roam

But as Responsibility feasts
And Apathy starts to grow
Boredom's roots get tangled
Stifled and stagnant.
Burning under blue light streams
They wither and fade
Until they are nothing more than...

Mourning,
Imagination, mourning
The loss of Youth and Boredom
Goes to find Time
to see if they can do something.
But Time moves slower than you think
And faster than one wants
And Imagination finds that
Boredom has a new best friend

Memory
The mighty three
Together for eternity
Youth, Boredom, and Memory
Trapped peacefully in the
Privileged web of
Rest

## Spicket

Flint STILL doesn't have clean drinking water
   And they're hosing the concrete down
A Cockroach carcass decays on my stairway
   And they're hosing the concrete down
Hurricanes sweeping away
generational health, Chlorine clouds
Soundproof windows muffle
A poverty stricken howl
Naively in their towers
   Their concrete gets hosed down
   High pressured preferred
   To wash away the doubts
They used to hose down my people
   At least it's just concrete now
The long shore man are striking
The students are kicked out
Capital society is crumbling
   As they hose the concrete down
The concrete is bombed on families
Or they starve them out
   Colonizing cucks love watching
   As they hose the concrete down
Community resources dried up
   As they hose the concrete down
The watering holes priced out

Because they hose the concrete down
Kidnapped and tortured
Industrial prison labor abound
Can't get the blood off our hands

So hose the concrete down

## Root Rot

I've been conditioned to believe that more is
Better
When, in fact,
Different
is better than Better because
Different is
Knowledge
And I cannot bring myself to be ignorant
Can't let my tree atrophy
Can't over water
Can't have my roots rot

I over do it
Pour into others
leaving myself depleted
leaving the other party rotten
Sopping wet with love
I didn't keep for myself
I sit soaking in grace self-afforded
Intolerant to drought
Dripping in dreams hopes promises
While the DMs dry
The roots rot

I over do it
Let the dough rest
Too long too flat
Stretched too thin
carbon dioxide overproduction
Bubbling over
Suffocating in my self care
Stagnating in my Haj
Idle in my garage
Shears snip off the yellow leaves
Of decaying seasons change
Deciduous forest floor fertilizing
New age artistry
Circle of life balancing
The finality of mortality
Antiseptic sterilized
Cauterized
Laying down the healing waters

## Hand Me Downs

I put you in the shirt he left behind to see if it fits
Does it hang off of you?Does it hug your shoulders like it did
his?Are you swimming in it?Is it restricting your airways?Are you
drowning in his shoes?

I put you in his shirt to see if it fits
Is that fabric a little          more                    breathable?
Can you see this as a wardrobe staple
Inhabiting his brand
This perfect model of


                              him

I put you in his shirt
Behind drawn curtains
and you wore his hand-me downs well
Our thriftiness obvious
to no one except those
With a keen eye for fashion

Habits ✓
Warnings ✓
Patterns ✓
Symptoms ✓

You were a walking medical chart
His shirt a hospital gown
Your body an open cavity
Echoing out my insecurities

I put you in his shirt
It fit you like a glove
A goldilocks moment
Like magic
one and a billion odds

I put you in the shirt he left behind and you became him
                        An apparition
A Phantom
                                A "once was" distant thought
A possibility
                                            A never stood a chance

Gone
But not forgotten
Airbrushed onto a t-shirt with Angel wings
I put you in his shirt
And you followed in his footsteps
Leaving yours behind

## Molotov

Glass half full
Innovation that ignites
White flags feign submission
Shooting stars across the sky

Bottle half full
Incendiary flight
Frangible vessels
Fired up for our rights

Streets half full
Fuses set alight
Arm cocked back
Rebellion in their eyes

Shop windows full
Of flaming patrons' plight
Capitalistic consciousness
Burns from molotovs at night

## Birthday

Mama said
I was born on a day
and it wasn't yesterday
For myself I can't say for certain
But I think I've been born again
More than again
Baptized by fire
The birthday of the phoenix

I've been grieving while celebrating
A mother finally lives for herself
So far from home
Umbilical cord stretching thin
Cross continental connection

I have a birthday this Friday
I've been laboring for months but
Friday is when I'm due
When the invisible umbilical is severed
And a copper iou is placed

It's going to be a home birth homecoming
A waterborne waterboarding of wisdom
Maternal metamorphosis
Planting of perennials

My mother has migrated
To the land of her own
But she ain't alone

I left you for my dreams
And you left for something easy

**Dandelion's Destiny** ✳

Being blown apart

By the gentlest of winds

Those seeds taking root

Being blown apart again

Being a dandelion
is to be destined

## Superwoman

There's been an eerie silence surrounding me
As I try to find my voice in a falling empire
A bubble of fibreglass insulation slicing my lungs
As muted footfalls descend into madness.

Been too depressed to write anything good
Or what I perceive to be good
It never feels like enough.
Scraping the bottom of the container of frosting
To embellish my bitter emotions so they are easier to swallow
A spoonful of sugar, to help the truth go down.

I've poured my heart out
With nothing in return but hesitant hand claps
And pitifully empty pockets.
So I'm going to stop pretending I'm not weary.

Underneath this decoration and decoupage
Is disappointment
I'm numb, hazy jaded dissipated
I wish I could perform exclusively for play
And not survival. I'm running
Out of ways to say
We should be treated better.

## Benediction

Before I pass away
If I shall pass at all
I want you to grieve me
while I'm young
Have my celebration of life
before it flashes before me
Let it be a party of glitter
Mirror balls reflecting your mortality
Streamers with the names of my lovers and loved ones
Cascading above

Prior to my funeral pyre
Promise me you will learn my histories
Recite my poems and read my diaries
Ruminate on my words
Traverse the earth to find the place of my modeling clay
Shape it
Into bowls and plates
Serve those who served me
And feast on my flesh
rendering out the fat that made me
full of life and laughter
Eat until your bellies are swollen and the itis
Creeps in
Swaddle yourself in the cloth I was cut from

Rest your eyes on the sunset you'll find me in

All I ask of you is to
Grieve me while I'm young
Before my ears deafen to the applause
And sweet nothings turn into silence
While I'm able to still tend to my garden
Give me my flowers
That I may watch them bloom
And turn their fragrant petals into perfumes
The smell of memory and petricor
Of nights spent staring at the sky
For the dreams and stars I shot for

If you must, grieve while I'm still here
Do it loudly and bold
Profess your love or disdain
to every person who dares to listen
To learn the legend of The Legend
The keeper of the Grove
Turn the fruits of my labor
into preserves, jams and jellies
So that I may linger tacky
where my name is laid

Amen

*Forgiving*

## Magnet Mixtape #1- Weird Fishes

i.
Black Is the Colour of My True Love's Hair
b i g f e e l i n g s Bless Me
Black Is The Circle Manaok (Forbidden)

ii.
NAna's iNteRlude Ballad No.9
Tell Me Long Ears Hear The Bells
alright My Song Hearts A Mess

iii.
Is Your Love Big Enough?
Open 6 8 Sula (Paperback) boxes
One Calls
Come as You Are
I Want You Around Another Lifetime

iv.
Fruitflies Satellite
Green Papaya Hemispheres
Where Do You Go
Waiting Room - Demo reprise

v.

Woman (feat. Lianne La Havas)
She Milk & Honey Rainforest LiGht For Granted
The Chain Orbit HiPs
Thin Line. Float Yellow Story
She. Make It Holy
One (of A Kind). Modern Soul
Have Mercy

vi.

Doubt Quarrel
Colouour Out the Lies
Don't Wake Me Up

vii.

Bittersweet Bottom of the River
Water No Get Enemy
Weird Fishes Stranger/ Lover Lotus Blossom
Lovely Intermission Hunger
Those Good Times Indulge Me

## Cassandra

I'm ought to name my gut
Cassandra
I should have known better
Felt better
Acted accordingly…..
But I don't know how to listen
The knot twisting in the pit
Of my pooch pushed out puppy sniffin
Cassandra said I was hard headed
Hard hearted too
Lissstennn
Somethin is in the air
Persons missin
Somethings amiss in there
Cassandra is growling
Miss girl is gurglin
She's intuitin but

I

Ain't

Listenin

Puppy sniffin

If it ain't sittin right with your spirit
it ain't it
Listen to Cassandra, Mama
She knows what going on
Barkin up a midnight storm
Toss and flip you off
Keep you from sleepin
Back slidin into bad habit keepin
Cassandra
always with the damn drama
Shut the fuck up
And stop bitchin

## Eve of 100

On the eve,
you'd think you'd sync with the moon
in all her glory
her grandeur, her brightness,
reflecting your own.
Her light emanating from within

On the eve,
night
viscous and thick
wading through the air
legs leaden
The end of your marathon
The evening before your finale,
anticipating metamorphosis,
itching to become holier than before
clear and precise,
a vector invested

yet on that very eve you feel
the future opaque with options
opportunities, chances
paths like heaping plates of spaghetti
A shuffled deck

there is anxiety in the eve
no proof in the pudding,
 just plain tapioca
An arrangement of dissonance
bows but playing a familiar tune to
strange audience.

Transfiguration doesn't happen overnight
cocoon sweltering
sweat sloughing off impatient impurity

Change was never supposed to be comfortable
Easy. The alchemist on the eve
throwing it all at the wall
Seeing what from the past one hundred will stick
What bonds have formed
gold spun
Elixir sipped and dribbled down chin
Elements
of surprise.
A stillborn thought
A copper IOU
Ectopic developments, discoveries,
Disco balls and Disconnect.

throat chakra opens wide
when chemical cauterization ceases

poison as the prize
pain as the promise
projectile, as the punishment
Timeline of smooth edges
life in pieces
Repaired, replayed.

On the eve of one hundred days,
The moon is a beacon at the end
of sobriety celebrity's ego death.
Chapter closer cliff hanger

Who lies on the other side?

**Imani**

My namesake, homegirl
        Mover of needles
        Bearer of grief
The World's light
        Spilling into the folds of
        My everyday
patience and acceptance

Imani
The believer
The over-stander
        The "to their own detrimental-"
Faith
She will prevail
Ruminating in her healing
        Fingers fixing crowns
Chasing dreams in butterfly nets
        And cobwebs

Imani
        The ancient
All knowing
Secret holder
Stronger
Than acrylic nails, wax

        Strips
Ego, Eco-styler gel on
4C edges
On a hot day
At higghhh noon

Imani
The mirror
The coin
Flipped into fountain
Water
Flowing
        and
            Falling
                To cool
           pools
        below

Imani
Mourning
        And Knight
        Shining

**Bald Headed**

Never in my life have I been bald headed
Balding or bald spotted
My shit been thique
I came out screaming with my head full
With quizzical coils
With A microphone
With a Dandelion's mane

I was born bearing an eclipse
shape shifters gift
disguise to prying eyes

I often wish I was born without
Wish I knew how to love
Without woolen security blanket

Scalped bald
Vulnerable dimpled
exposed
An embryonic love

**The Grove**

The Grove
can be painted for hefty payment
Or maintained
for far less

So I'll dirty my hands
with moss poles and soil
for I don't mind the mess

And I'll grow new life
From bulbs and cuttings,
To help me cope
With my short time with you

The Grove will beautify
my dark spots
with fresh green sprouts
with golden flowers bloomed

## Cake Tiers

Every year I cry on my birthday
It's cathartic at this point
Expected
I flush out the past year through my tear ducts
Disappointments
Detours and details
Birthday cake tiers
tasting of gluttonous guilt
Notes of the life I should have lived
and grief from the one I did.
This year I wept for all
my prayers
Answered and deferred
For missed opportunities
and exercising all options.
Birthday cake tiers fall
for ganache goodnights
Filled with caramel jazz cries
For friendships well fed and famished
Birthday cake tiers of joy
For another trip around the sun.

## 4:15 Insomnimania

Insomnimania
It's not quite insomnia.
I can sleep
just not at night
At night
My spirit comes alive
suckling at the silence of the witching hours.
My soul communes with the Moon
Pores sweating
as the morning dew brews

Insomnimania
thoughts growing with the shadows
shrouded in supple isolation,
me, my thoughts, and the sky.
A Nocturnal narrator
A woman of the night
hushed howls scribbled
to calm the swimming
images that crowd
My bustling brain
Words need to have their freedom too
stroke of the pen, ink bleeding
through pages, down the wall,
Into skin

Insomnimania
What should I get for my next tattoo?
Should I take melatonin for productive daylight function?
Smoke a bowl, floating into dusky intermission?
Default back to factory settings?
No
I am fully customized
from my digs to my tint
Claws Snatching prayers
Now I lay me down to sleep
I hear the upstairs floorboard's creak.
Maybe I'm awake
because I forgot to eat

Insomnimania
Ideas just keep coming
a steady flow.
In one ear, out the other
rapid-fire findings
caught between down pillows
emerge through pen and paper.
~~{I wrote a squiggle here}~~
This is a rough draft.
Brainstorm clouds rolling in
thunder and lightning, but no rain.

It must be summer

somewhere.

## Bantu Baby

Bantu knot baby
Bent over bathtub faucet
Soapy eyed and scared
I will always do your hair
Wipe the oceans from your cheeks
Teach you a tune
And listen
As you howl at the moon

Bantu knot baby
Whose loss eclipses mine
Whose troubles I can't tuck away
Whose problems I can't plait back
And make presentable
Respectable

Bantu knot baby
Whose edges I won't tame
Whose hands mimic mine
Whose journey I can't walk
I will grease your scalp
detangle your thoughts
with wide toothed tenderness
Swaddle you in satin
And listen
As you howl at the moon

## Hair on the Bathroom Floor

You're still here.
Maybe not fully
But I find pieces of you
Left behind
In the minds of lovers
Friends, follicles
In colors of the fruit stand
In smiles of strangers
In the words of
Each play performed
I'm still finding
Your hair on the bathroom floor
The coils
Sticking to the tile
The corners of the room
Always watching
The colors change
With the season
The 1b, auburn
Ice spice
Each a different time
Each a different you
But little one
In this body
Now

Carrying the ache
The weight of
Timeless tendrils
The people you
Are no longer
But always will be
Clean house often
Thank your crown
For shaping you
Then sweep it away

## Cured

Cover me in salt
and throw me in the freezer

Cover me with sugar
and keep away the flies

Cover me in smoke
for hours on end

Cover me in prayers
until I see you again

**Sweet Thang**

I can feel myself getting soft again.
This popsicle heart thawing as we enter her season
Butter folding into Brown sugar, chocolate chips, macaronage
flour child of gingerbread
buttercream dream, spirit of stiff peaks and marshmallow wafers of forgiveness,
broken bread peace treaty.

I can feel myself getting soft again
like ballerina's gliding.
Like smoke hovering over head
like down blankets and pillow forts
semester sisters away.
Weight of hardcover novels
Like meadows of a new world.
Like leaves unfurling
a natural presentation.
A mating ritual exposing oneself to self love.

I'm getting soft again
like an open wound gushing jelly filled enjoyable.
I can feel myself getting soft again.
I can feel myself being soft again.
After having hardened off for brutal winter's chill,
I feel music, feeling joy without feeling remorse or guilt or glory.

I feel myself becoming myself again.
I can feel myself softening out of PVC pipe rice crispy treat structures
I'm not just beautiful on the outside
I taste good too
I comfort like angel food cake, strawberries and cream
I bake Myself
Rise and transform out of butter sugar and flour into
Manna from heaven.
I am stardust reconstructed.
To all the other bakers
whose hands have pounded and kneaded me
and so many open hands have needed me
I still stand
reinforced, layered, crumb coat even.

I can feel myself getting soft again.
And what a crazy feeling it is to want to be consumed

*For Living*

## Magnet Mixtape #2- Ummm... I guess

i.

Window Raisin' Granny Fly Away
Everybody Loves The Sunshine
Can You Get To That Milk N' Honey What Is Hip?
Open Country Joy
Once in a Lifetime Thing

ii.

Hunger Under Control Without You
Overnight California Dreamin'
Seven Prayers Heavy, California Métropole Flight
I Want You Back Maiysha (So Long)

iii.

Afro Blue Brother, I'm Hungry

Bad Kids To The Back

It's Not the Crime

Change of The Guard
Ride or die (feat. Foster the People)

iv.

Aunt Leslie Wesley's Theory
Never Change Lovers in the Middle of The Night
Shofukan Soundgirl Personal
I Like It Like That

v.
It's a New Day
Yellow Story Since I Had You
Such a Night Drops
His Eye is On The Sparrow Space of You


vi.
Strawberry Letter 23
Nineteen Seventy Something
Good Morning Neighbor
Working Man Dr. Funk Tubaluba Tadow
Won't Be Coming back
So Very Hard to Go
Thanks For Your Time
Your Love is Mine


vii.
You Don't Know Verve Weird Fishes
Street Fighter Mas Liquid Love Drips
Quick Seven Hours With A Backseat Driver
Roll With It
The Lemon Song Bittersweet
How Deep Is Your Love?

viii.

Beware The Groove At The Foot Of Canal Street
Tuba Fats Bright Lights
Piazole Tramp - Mono Feelin' Alright
I Don't Mind The Dark Streets Miss Modular
I Want You
Flashlight I'll Take You There

**Velcro**

Two little girls sit on the A train
One writes in her little journal (very seriously)
The older one reads a book aloud
Neither can tie their shoes yet
The younger one doesn't realize
her sister voice is the one she'll turn to
for comfort in foreign lands
were silver serpentine creatures snake through the city
The older one doesn't know
she'll look to her sister for guidance
A hand drawn map of the unexpected.
The perfect word to describe moment after moment
shared between velcro straps
Neither can tie their shoes yet
And they retreat into their own worlds
Their own heads
Unable, unwilling to untie the knot they share

**Facecard**

I can't believe it
I woke up today
And saw a brand new face!
How peculiar
I thought at my big age
I would have seen them all
Each a different etching, iteration
Of Mom, Dad, siblings
Classmates coworkers
And You
From past lives
Every Karmic reincarnation
I saw the face of God
The first time I held the sky
Future and legacy
Reflected back to me
And yet
today I saw a new face
How strange
To look somebody in the face
To extract every clogged pore
Contour, shadow and gloss
To watch them blink
Wink cry
I've seen all of those before but

Today I saw yours
Isula in a sea of seen
Of been there done that
Let's face the facts
I saw a new face today

**Hypothesis**

Have you ever had a well fed friendship?
I did some research and
My Hypothesis
Is so fine
Her mind is on a different level
Her capacity for love is on a different level

Empress Empirical
Clocking the tea before the water boils
"Yes, and "
All while holding hands

My Hypothesis
Is a Bad Bitch
Stomps her feet to the beat of her own drum
Dances through her own
Arrhythmia and Blues

Thought daughter
Globe Trotter
One of one

My If Then
Dream Catcher and Curator
Confident Confidant

My Hypothesis
Is headed to a land all her own
Hunting and gathering her joys along the way
Thank goddess she picked me

## Terracotta

I wrap myself
With your residue drops
Wrinkled sheets and fitful sleeps
Inside
Terracotta duvet
Vines sprout
From restless legs

Thai red curry
Spicy sweet
Lobster and bread
Eggplant stew
Droplets on a back sink
Coconut milk
Bamboo shoot

Terracotta
Earthenware
Heavy Porous Planter
Duvet Pot Clay
Unglazed
Fired
Iron oxide
Secondary
Imperfection impurities

Bricks tiles sculptures
Soldiers
Rough sanded
Natural

Terracotta bed sheets beckon
My body hurts
I lose my appetite
As I finish making
Spicy Italian breakfast sandwich

I walk down my stairs
To retrieve neon parking ticket
Off of my windshield

Then I see you

and the Sun
For the first time in days
Finally comes out

**Imani "Faith" Imani "Saith"**

Just so you know we ended up down South
in the bayou with spanish moss
75 degree winters
Plastic beads and acrylic lacquer coconuts

The house is beautiful
White tiles and couches and carpets and concrete
There's a pot filler over the stove
And a deep sink in the island
And a small room with no real purpose
But to house the buffet tables when guests come over
You'll never get to see it

Writing things down might make them true
There is no real science to these sorts of things
Only faith or fear that God or the Universe or my atoms
will hear and act upon them
It's been years since we last spoke and I can't remember
The last words I spoke to you
I kept your voicemail of I love you
Dried out your bouquets to potpourri my pain
Do you still keep our photos close by?

I'm sorry I didn't let you take me down South
Fear a blindfold to the fullness of you

Of your community of your care
I remember now
It was about death
You didn't offer condolences

Your Mother's paintings
hang in the home of mine
She styled an entire room around them
A diptych
I held on to them incase you came back
You'll never get to see it

## Cuppa

If you can't go to sleep
You must make a cuppa
To make a cuppa
You need to boil water
No kettle or stove needed
Just one mug of water
Preferably your favorite mug
In the microwave for 3 minutes
As the hum from the microwave
Mimics your hungry tummy
You must consider
All the loose leaf options
Your pantry has to offer
When you snap out of
Decision making dilemma
You should choose
Lavender, chamomile, mint
For cozy sleepy stomach sedating
The microwave will wail
3 times to be exact
And you must retrieve
Your steaming mug of possibility
You put your potpourri in
A mesh baptism bag
And let it steep

You must let the sleep steep in
Sweeten to your liking
And keep steeping
And steeping
Until
You are sleeping

## 6:20 Insomnimania

i.
Sometimes you fast from
Instead of falling fast to
Sunrise gold thread count

ii.
Of all my notebooks
Of all my hurried etchings
I long for disco

iii.
My thoughts bested me
Scrambling words at quarter past
My hair should be done

iv.
Pasta and meatballs
Plucked ripe with gilded talons
My plants keep dying

v.
Abstain and Abstain
Please I'm begging you Abstain
For your sake and mine

## Optical Illusion

What I do isn't powerful
It's precious
Soul refracting through
The facets of a clenched
Gapped tooth smile
Fangs hang
Laughter stifled

What I do is not impressive
It's personal
It's just how I view the world
Pupils dilate with discovery
Salivate for something
Supple, fresh
In this life and the next
Pavlovian response

What I do isn't pure
It's an interpolation
Introspection
Condemnation
A liminal subject to be studied
Where does audacity
live in the body?

What I do isn't democratic
It's decadent deception
The hiss and sizzle
Of a decaying nation
Swing dancing
Swing votes
Pavlovian response

What I do is putrid
It isn't perfumed purge
Flowery language can't
Condone, cologne
history repeating itself

What I do isn't perfect
It's Pointillism
Privileged
Responsibility bestowed
Kighted with the pen
that's mightier than
Ring a bell?

What I do
And have always done
Is find peace in the panic
Wrestle with the mania
Of political propaganda

The pendulum must swing

What I do isn't projection
It's pond water
Ripples wrinkle
Time
Embeds itself into
Furtive furrowed brow

What I do isn't performance
It's a presentation
Slack jawed and honest
Recitation of my writes
Incantation of my duality

Propagation of the Garden
Of Eden
A praxis of paradise
Liberation from paralyzing
despondency

What I do is alchemize
Apathy into Empathy
Empathy into Action
Action into Reciprocity
I can't unring this bell

What I do is an
Optical Illusion
Polka dotted
Pavlovian
Checker boarded
Stairs to nowhere
Warped and contorted
Inquiry
Where does wisdom hide in the body?

## Tiny Pink Eraser

Of all of the tools at my disposal
Paper, pencil, pen
I'd like to be
the tiny pink eraser
at the other end.
~~You see, my words~~
~~My words~~
Words
get lost sometimes
In translation or interpolation.
Ink bleeds and the blessings
blotted out of memory.
Graphite smudges,
Snaps under society's pressure
Every idea must be a diamond.
It's performance anxiety
Borderline insanity
To be a productive number–
MEMBER of a society
that's never produced shit for me.
So I coast.

A tiny pink eraser
Crowd surfing on the shoulders of
trailblazers and trend setters

Making their marks.
Only taking me as far as their
Words and worlds will carry.
What quotes I can remember
What names I can drop
What Bible verse can I chew,
spit back out and stick my message to.

Pen, pencil paper
I can't rely on unreliable narrator
Orator
Memory is illusive.
Folks are forgetful
about what happens in the middle.
Which facts are in fact facts
What secrets seductively spilled
Unable to decipher the
Influx of inflammatory information.
Forced to read between
illegible college ruled ledgers.
Mistakes struck from records
Lines crossed, lives lost

Redacted
The oppressors–victors
write the history books.
Worlds are lost

In translation, by bastardization.
The hand that launched
a thousand censorships.
Of all of the tools at my disposal
Paper, pencil, pen.
I'll be the tiny pink eraser
Who tells the story at the end.

Let me be the editor
A reviser– advisor.
Let me route out redundancy,
accentuate accomplishment.
Let me pore over the truth
resinous and insatiable.
Let me get to the point
Sharpend, honed in
The moral of this story isn't at the start
It's at the other end
The tiny pink eraser
wields more power
than the pen.

*About the Mixtapes*

*Magnet Mixtape* is an ongoing project highlighting lost mediums of affection. Historically mixtapes were given to crushes, friends, and even family to share in the revelry of music and community; To express emotions shared, a musical love letter. The songs were often arranged in a way that took the listeners on a journey, deepening the connection between curator and confidant. The storytelling order of the songs would spark conversation and debate within the listening party, extend into the greater community, creating the culture of content sharing. Today, sharing music no longer requires an in-person exchange. With the digitization of most media, streamed playlists have become popularized over the physical mixtape and discussion takes place in online spaces.

Modernization is taking over traditional aspects within the home as well. Of all the appliances that could signify one's affluence, or lack thereof, refrigerators have become that status symbol. White refrigerators are seen as a circumstance of being impoverished (thank you Nene Leakes) causing folks to opt for sleek, homogenous stainless steel options. These chrome appliances are often characterless and the heart of the home lacks in soul. Its glossy exterior only reflects back the external image of the home's inhabitants while the internal lives are hidden away for fear of being seen ( "we can't let people know we sit"). The vivid magnets that once hung proudly on refrigerators highlighting travels and past lives are no longer present to serve as a point of entry into familial histories. This widens the disconnect between generations as there is no tactile way to connect with the past in everyday life.

Joining together the tradition of mixtape sharing and refrigerator magnet poetry, *Magnet Mixtape* hopes to reframe the way we interact with the content we consume daily and the stories we share with loved ones. *Magnet Mixtape 1 & 2* are crafted from playlists shared between coworkers. A peek into lives outside of the workplace to view the humanity of the individuals in forced proximity to one another. Maya invites the reader to listen to these playlists and evaluate how they show affection to the people and art in which they surround themselves.

## Umm… I Guess?

## Weird Fishes

# *Acknowledgements*

✳ ✳ ✳

To my ancestors Andrea, Denyse, Diane, John, Van, Wayne, William, and Zinzinita, thank you for providing me with love and legacy.

To my siblings, you are the reasons I go so hard.

To my parents, I would be nothing without your support, love and acceptance.

To Dakarai for being my one phone call away. Without you this book wouldn't have gotten finished.

Annie, Ilana, Joel, Jordan, Max, Rayne, Shiku, the space you hold for me has allowed for a growth unimaginable. I am in awe of you all.

✳ ✳ ✳

And to you, My Reader,
Thank you for allowing me to entrust my words with you.